SPANISH
WORKBOOK
FOR GRADES 1, 2, AND 3

**140+ LANGUAGE LEARNING
EXERCISES FOR KIDS**

Melanie Stuart-Campbell

callisto
publishing
an imprint of Sourcebooks

For all the teachers, parents, and children who value learning a new language. *Sí, se puede.*

Published by Callisto Publishing LLC C/O Sourcebooks LLC
P.O. Box 4410, Naperville, Illinois 60567-4410
(630) 961-3900
callistopublishing.com

This product conforms to all applicable CPSC and CPSIA standards.

Source of Production: Wing King Tong Paper Products Co.Ltd. Shenzhen, Guangdong Province, China
Date of Production: April 2024
Run Number: 5039296

Printed and bound in China
WKT 3

CONTENTS

Note to Parents and Teachers iv

Note to Parents and Teachers

¡Hola! Thank you for choosing this book to teach your kids early bilingual skills. This is the best time to introduce a new language, as the brain is most receptive at a young age. Learning an additional language offers many benefits, including improved problem-solving, critical thinking, and listening skills, to name just a few.

This book includes 144 Spanish language exercises for grades 1, 2, and 3. Your child will learn many skills and concepts, ranging from the alphabet and common words to more advanced greetings and grammar.

The lessons are color-coded by grade to help you find the appropriate activities. Each concept is introduced in an easy-to-understand format, including how to correctly pronounce the words in Spanish. The more kids *say* the words out loud, the better, so please encourage them to speak frequently. The exercises advance in difficulty as the book progresses, so I recommend starting with the first lesson for each grade level. However, if your learner has prior experience with Spanish, feel free to skip to a lesson that is more challenging.

I am thrilled to share this book with you and your learners, as teaching Spanish is one of my passions. I have over 25 years of experience teaching languages and this is my fifth published book about learning *español.* Have fun!

Grade 1

1. Counting 1 to 10

Say each word.
Then write the Spanish word.

1. uno [OO-noh]

_____

2. dos [DOHS]

_____

3. tres [TREHS]

_____

4. cuatro [koo-AH-troh]

_____

5. cinco [SEEN-koh]

_____

6. seis [SEH-ees]

_____

7. siete [see-EH-teh]

_____

8. ocho [OH-choh]

_____

9. nueve [noo-EH-veh]

_____

10. diez [dee-EHS]

_____

2. Counting 11 to 20

Say each word.
Then write the Spanish word.

---

11. once [OHN-seh]

12. doce [DOH-seh]

13. trece [TREH-seh]

14. catorce [kah-TOHR-seh]

15. quince [KEEN-seh]

16. dieciséis [dee-eh-see-SEH-ees]

17. diecisiete [dee-eh-see-see-EH-teh]

18. dieciocho [dee-eh-see-OH-choh]

19. diecinueve [dee-eh-see-noo-EH-veh]

20. veinte [VEH-een-teh]

3. Counting Balloons

Say each word.
Then write the number.

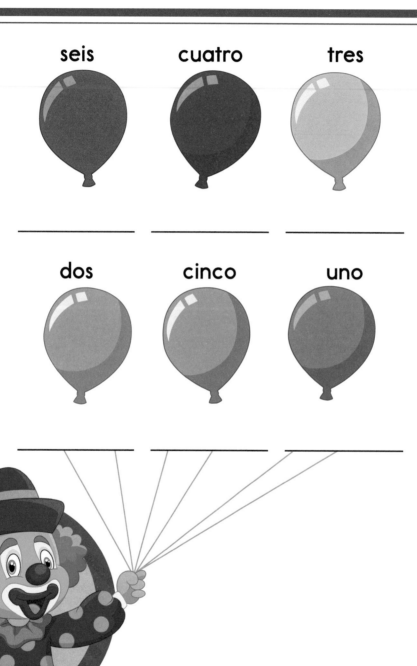

seis

cuatro

tres

_____ _____ _____

dos

cinco

uno

_____ _____ _____

4. Which Number?

Say each word.
Then circle the matching number.

catorce	4 14 13
doce	2 15 12
quince	15 5 16
veinte	2 20 7
diecisiete	13 17 19
once	5 18 11
dieciocho	14 18 16
trece	13 15 3
dieciséis	14 16 6
diecinueve	9 19 11

5. Letters in Spanish

Say each letter from the Spanish alphabet.
Then write three words using the letters on this page.

A [AH]

B [BEH]

C [SEH]

CH [CHEH]

D [DEH]

E [EH]

F [EH-feh]

G [HEH]

H [AH-cheh]

I [EE]

J [HOH-tah]

K [KAH]

L [EH-leh]

LL [EH-yeh]

M [EH-meh]

6. More Spanish Letters

Say each letter from the Spanish alphabet.
Then write three words using the letters on this page.

N [EH-neh]

Ñ [EH-nyeh]

O [OH]

P [PEH]

Q [KOO]

R [EH-reh]

RR [EH-rreh]

S [EH-seh]

T [TEH]

U [OO]

V [VEH]

W [DOH-bleh-veh]

X [EH-kees]

Y [YEH]

Z [SEH-tah]

7. Name the Letters

Say the Spanish word for each number. Then write the word. Say each letter as you write it.

2

4

6

8

10

8. Letters and Sounds

Draw a line from each number to the first sound of the Spanish word.

7

13

9

8

1

U

T

O

S

N

9. Write the Days

Say the Spanish word for each day of the week.
Then write the word.

MONDAY

lunes [LOO–nehs] _____

TUESDAY

martes [MAHR-tehs] _____

WEDNESDAY

miércoles [mee-EHR-koh-lehs] _____

THURSDAY

jueves [hoo-EH-behs] _____

FRIDAY

viernes [bee-EHR-nehs] _____

SATURDAY

sábado [SAH-bah-doh] _____

SUNDAY

domingo [doh-MEEN-goh] _____

10. Missing Days

Fill the blanks with the Spanish word for the next day of the week. Say the word as you write it.

lunes _____

miércoles _____

viernes _____

domingo _____

martes _____

jueves _____

sábado _____

11. Mixed-Up Days

Unscramble the days of the week.
Say each word as you write it.

1. abásod _____

2. nlseu _____

3. sevuje _____

4. rasmte _____

5. réslemoci _____

6. gimodon _____

7. srieenv _____

12. Ana's Week

Read Ana's calendar. Then write the answer to each question in Spanish. Say the word as you write it.

LUNES	MARTES	MIÉRCOLES	JUEVES	VIERNES	SÁBADO	DOMINGO
Go to the dentist	Clean my room	Do my laundry	Wash the dog	My birthday	My party	María's birthday

1. What day of the week is María's birthday?

   _____

2. What day of the week does Ana clean her room?

   _____

3. What day of the week does Ana go to the dentist?

   _____

4. What day of the week does Ana have a party?

   _____

5. What day of the week is Ana's birthday?

   _____

6. What day of the week does Ana do laundry?

   _____

7. What day of the week does Ana wash her dog?

   _____

13. A Year in Spanish

Say the Spanish word for each month of the year.
Then write the word.

JANUARY

enero [eh-NEH-roh]

_____

FEBRUARY

febrero [feh-BREH-roh]

_____

MARCH

marzo [MAHR-soh]

_____

APRIL

abril [ah-BREEL]

_____

MAY

mayo [MAH-yoh]

_____

JUNE

junio [HOO-nee-oh]

_____

JULY

julio [HOO-lee-oh]

_____

AUGUST

agosto [ah-GOHS-toh]

_____

SEPTEMBER

septiembre [sehp-tee-EHM-breh]

_____

OCTOBER

octubre [ohk-TOO-breh]

_____

NOVEMBER

noviembre [noh-vee-EHM-breh]

_____

DECEMBER

diciembre [dee-see-EHM-breh]

_____

14. Ana's Year Begins

Read Ana's calendar. Then write the answer to each question in Spanish. Say the word as you write it.

ENERO	FEBRERO	MARZO	ABRIL	MAYO	JUNIO
Happy New Year	Valentine's Day	My birthday	Visit my cousins	Mother's Day	Father's Day

1. What month is Father's Day?

   _____

2. What month is Ana's birthday?

   _____

3. What month does Ana visit her cousins?

   _____

4. What month is Mother's Day?

   _____

5. What month is New Year's Day?

   _____

6. What month is Valentine's Day?

   _____

15. Ana's Year Continues

Read Ana's calendar. Then write the answer to each question in Spanish. Say the word as you write it.

JULIO	AGOSTO	SEPTIEMBRE	OCTUBRE	NOVIEMBRE	DICIEMBRE
Go to the beach	Start school	Visit grandparents	Go to the doctor	Dad's birthday	Uncle Mario's wedding

1. What month is Ana's dad's birthday?

   _____

2. What month is Uncle Mario's wedding?

   _____

3. What month does Ana visit her grandparents?

   _____

4. What month does school start?

   _____

5. What month does Ana go to the beach?

   _____

6. What month does Ana go to the doctor?

   _____

16. Mixed-Up Months

Unscramble the months.
Say each word as you write it.

1. recidibem _____

2. nuioj _____

3. crotbue _____

4. breefor _____

5. togaso _____

6. mebrpetise _____

7. yoma _____

8. lioju _____

9. onree _____

10. razom _____

11. renobmeiv _____

12. brail _____

17. Colors All around Us

Say the colors in Spanish.
Then write which color is your favorite.

rojo
[ROH-hoh]

anaranjado
[ah-nah-rahn-HAH-doh]

amarillo
[ah-mah-REE-yoh]

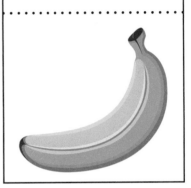

verde
[BEHR-deh]

azul
[ah-ZOOL]

morado
[moh-RAH-doh]

My favorite color on this page is: _____.

18. Color Your World

Say the colors in Spanish.
Then write which color is your favorite.

rosado
[roh-SAH-doh]

negro
[NEH-groh]

blanco
[BLAHN-koh]

café
[KAH-feh]

gris
[GREES]

My favorite color on this page is: _____.

19. Color the Flowers

Say each word.
Then color each flower to match the word.

morado

azul

amarillo

rojo

rosado

anaranjado

20. Color the Shirts

Say each word.
Then color each shirt to match the word.

negro   blanco   gris

verde   café

21. Match the Colors

Draw a line from each Spanish color to the matching English color. Use the color of the matching words to draw each line.

morado	white
azul	black
amarillo	purple
rojo	green
rosado	brown
anaranjado	blue
negro	yellow
blanco	red
gris	pink
verde	orange
café	gray

22. Over the Rainbow

Color each part of the rainbow
to match the word.

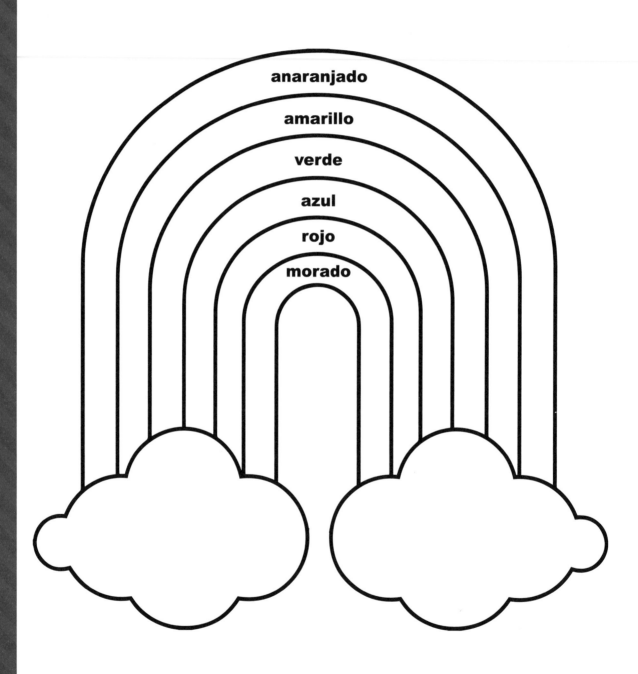

anaranjado

amarillo

verde

azul

rojo

morado

23. Hello and Goodbye

Say the Spanish words.
Then trace the words.

Hola / Hello	Adiós / Goodbye
[OH-lah]	[ah-dee-OHS]

Hola

Hola

Adiós

Adiós

24. Morning, Afternoon, and Evening

Say the Spanish words. Then trace the words.

Buenos días / Good morning	Buenas tardes / Good afternoon	Buenas noches / Good evening / night
[boo-EH-nohs-DEE-ahs]	[boo-EH-nahs-TAHR-dehs]	[boo-EH-nahs-NOH-chehs]

Buenos días   Buenos días

Buenas tardes   Buenas tardes

Buenas noches   Buenas noches

25. Match the Greetings

Draw a line from each Spanish greeting to
the matching English greeting.

Hola   Good evening/night

Adiós   Hello

Buenos días   Good afternoon

Buenas tardes   Good morning

Buenas noches   Goodbye

26. Fill in the Greetings

Look at each picture. Then write the missing letters for each greeting. Use the word bank to help you spell.

B__en__s
d__a__

__d__ __s

__u__ __as
__o__h__ __

WORD BANK

- Buenos días
- Buenas noches
- Adiós

GRADE 1: GREETINGS

27. El, La, Las, and Los

Spanish nouns are masculine/singular: el, masculine plural: los, feminine singular: la, or feminine plural: las.
Say the words. Then write the words in Spanish.

El taco
[EHL TAH-koh]

Los tacos
[LOHS TAH-kohs]

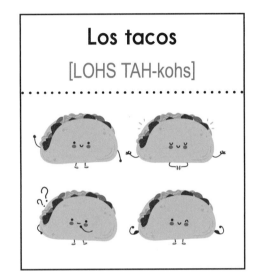

La vaca
[LAH BAH-kah]

Las vacas
[LAHS BAH-kahs]

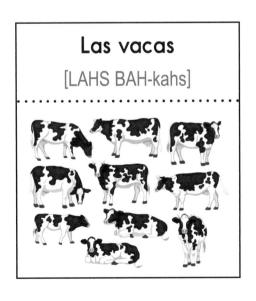

---

28. Missing Articles

Use the word bank to write the missing words.

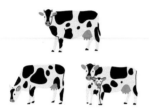

_____ vacas

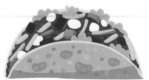

_____ taco

_____ vaca

_____ tacos

WORD BANK

● El ● La ● Las ● Los

29. Tracing the Face

Say the Spanish words. Then trace the words.

LAH KAH-ʀᴜʜ **FACE**

la cara   la cara

LOHS oh-HOS **EYES**

los ojos   los ojos

LAHS oh-RAY-has **EARS**

las orejas   las orejas

LAH nah-REEZ **NOSE**

la nariz   la nariz

LAH bo-KAH **MOUTH**

la boca   la boca

LOHS DEE-en-tehs **TEETH**

los dientes   los dientes

EHL kah-BEH-yoh **HAIR**

el cabello   el cabello

30. Say It Out Loud

Say the Spanish words.

el hombro [EHL OHM-broh] / shoulder

el brazo [EHL BRAH-soh] / arm

el codo [EHL KOH-doh] / elbow

la mano [LAH MAH-noh] / hand

el dedo de la mano [EHL DEH-doh DEH LAH MAH-noh] / finger

la pierna [LAH pee-EHR-nah] / leg

la rodilla [LAH roh-DEE-yah] / knee

el estómago [EHL ehs-TOH-mah-goh] / stomach

el pie [EHL pee-EH] / foot

el dedo del pie [EHL DEH-doh DEHL pee-EH] / toe

el cuerpo [EHL koo-EHR-poh] / body

31. Label the Face

Use the word bank to label the parts of the face.

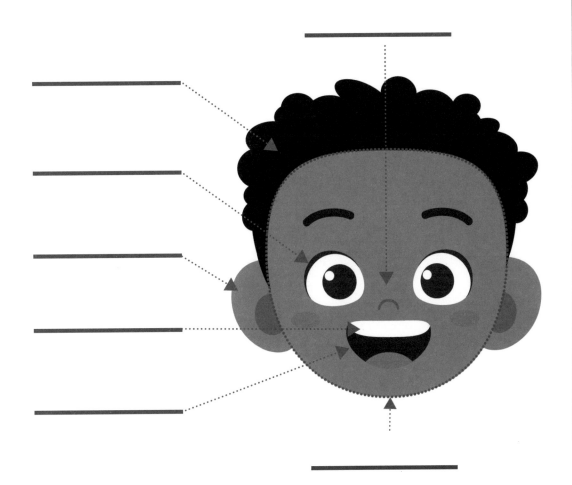

WORD BANK

- los ojos
- la cara
- el cabello
- la nariz
- la boca
- los dientes
- las orejas

32. Label the Body

Use the word bank to label the parts of the body.

WORD BANK

- el dedo de la mano
- la pierna
- la rodilla
- el estómago
- el hombro
- el brazo
- el codo
- la mano
- el cuerpo
- el pie
- el dedo del pie

33. Say and Trace Clothes

Say the Spanish words.
Then trace the words.

 LAH KAH-MEE-SAH **SHIRT**

la camisa | la camisa

 LAH GOH-rrah **CAP**

la gorra | la gorra

 LAH chah-KEH-tah **JACKET**

la chaqueta | la chaqueta

 LAH boo-FAHN-dah **SCARF**

la bufanda | la bufanda

 EHL soo-EHR-tehr **SWEATER**

el suéter | el suéter

 LOHS goo-AHN-tehs **GLOVES**

los guantes | los guantes

34. More Clothes

Say the Spanish words.
Then trace the words.

 EHL vehs-TEEH-doh **DRESS**

el vestido el vestido

 LOHS pahn-tah-LOH-nehs **PANTS**

los pantalones los pantalones

 EHL seen-tuh-ROHN **BELT**

el cinturón el cinturón

 LOHS sah-PAH-tohs **SHOES**

los zapatos los zapatos

 LOHS kahl-seh-TEEN-ehs **SOCKS**

los calcetines los calcetines

 LAHS BOH-tahs **BOOTS**

las botas las botas

35. Match the Clothes

Draw a line from each picture
to the matching words.

las botas

la chaqueta

los zapatos

los guantes

el cinturón

el suéter

36. Match More Clothes

Draw a line from each picture
to the matching words.

la gorra

la bufanda

la camisa

el vestido

los pantalones

los calcetines

37. What Would You Wear?

Write the answer to each clue in Spanish.

1. I wear these on my hands. _____

2. I wear these on my legs. _____

3. I wear this to hold my pants up. _____

4. I wear this around my neck when it's cold. _____

5. I wear these inside my shoes. _____

6. I wear this on my head. _____

38. Color the Clothing

Say the Spanish words. Then draw and color the clothing that matches the words.

| el vestido | el suéter | la chaqueta |

| la camisa | los zapatos | las botas |

39. Animal Fun

Say and write the words.
Then color the animals.

el perro	el gato	el pájaro
[EHL PEH-rroh]	[EHL GAH-toh]	[EHL PAH-hah-roh]

la serpiente	el pez	la vaca
[LAH sehr-pee-EHN-teh]	[EHL PEHS]	[LAH BAH-kah]

40. More Animals

Say and write the words.
Then color the animals.

el caballo	**el león**	**el tigre**
[EHL kah-BAH-yoh]	[EHL leh-OHN]	[EHL TEE-greh]

  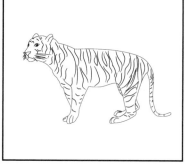

el oso	**el mono**	**la rana**
[EHL OH-soh]	[EHL MOH-noh]	[LAH RAH-nah]

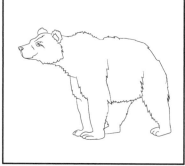  

41. Even More Animals

Say and write the words.
Then color the animals.

la abeja	el pato	la tortuga
[LAH ah-BEH-hah]	[EHL PAH-toh]	[LAH tohr-TOO-gah]

la mariposa	el elefante	el cerdo
[LAH mah-ree-POH-sah]	[EHL eh-leh-FAHN-teh]	[EHL SEHR-doh]

42. Match the Animals

Draw a line from each picture
to the matching words.

el perro

el gato

el pájaro

la serpiente

el pez

la vaca

43. Which Animal?

Write the answer to each clue in Spanish.
Then color the animals.

1. This land animal has no legs. _____

2. This animal barks. _____

3. This animal has gills. _____

4. This animal meows. _____

5. This animal flies. _____

6. This animal is white with black spots. _____

44. Animal Names

Write the name of each animal in Spanish. Use the word bank to help you spell. Then color the animals.

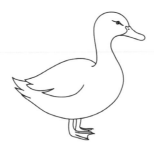

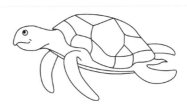

_____

_____

_____

_____

_____

_____

WORD BANK

• el elefante • la mariposa • el pato • el cerdo • la abeja • la tortuga

45. Animal Pictures

Draw and color the correct number of animals.

el oso

dos, café

la mariposa

diez, azul

la serpiente

trece, verde

el pez

ocho, anaranjado

el pájaro

seis, azul

el pato

tres, amarillo

46. Spell It in Spanish

Write the Spanish words that match each picture. Then say the letters in each word using the Spanish alphabet.

TUESDAY   Tuesday   _____

nose   _____

JANUARY   January   _____

feet   _____

MONDAY   Monday   _____

shirt   _____

SATURDAY   Saturday   _____

teeth   _____

47. Match the Words

Draw a line from the Spanish words to the matching English words.

los pantalones	ears
miércoles	leg
el caballo	Good morning
los ojos	March
Buenos días	pants
la pierna	Wednesday
marzo	horse
las orejas	eyes

48. Which Spanish Word?

Write the words in Spanish.
Use the word bank to help you spell.

1. Friday _____

2. gloves _____

3. Good afternoon _____

4. mouth _____

5. frog _____

6. Thursday _____

7. Good night _____

8. socks _____

9. stomach _____

10. December _____

WORD BANK

- jueves
- Buenas noches
- la rana
- los calcetines
- Buenas tardes
- viernes
- los guantes
- la boca
- diciembre
- el estómago

Grade 2

49. Numbers 21 to 30

Say each word.

GRADE 2: NUMBERS

21. veintiuno [veh-een-tee-OO-noh]

22. veintidós [veh-een-tee-DOHS]

23. veintitrés [veh-een-tee-TREHS]

24. veinticuatro [veh-een-tee-koo-AH-troh]

25. veinticinco [veh-een-tee-SEEN-koh]

26. veintiséis [veh-een-tee-SEH-ees]

27. veintisiete [veh-een-tee-see-EH-teh]

28. veintiocho [veh-een-tee-OH-choh]

29. veintinueve [veh-een-tee-noo-EH-veh]

30. treinta [TREH-een-tah]

50. Numbers 31 to 40

Say each word.

31. **treinta y uno** [TREH-een-tah-ee-OO-noh]

32. **treinta y dos** [TREH-een-tah-ee-DOHS]

33. **treinta y tres** [TREH-een-tah-ee-TREHS]

34. **treinta y cuatro** [TREH-een-tah-ee- koo-AH-troh]

35. **treinta y cinco** [TREH-een-tah-ee-SEEN-koh]

36. **treinta y seis** [TREH-een-tah-ee-SEH-ees]

37. **treinta y siete** [TREH-een-tah-ee-see-EH-teh]

38. **treinta y ocho** [TREH-een-tah-ee-OH-choh]

39. **treinta y nueve** [TREH-een-tah-ee-noo-EH-veh]

40. **cuarenta** [koo-ah-REHN-tah]

51. Which Number?

Say the words.
Then circle the matching number.

treinta y siete	37	27	36
veintiocho	22	28	29
cuarenta	40	14	34
treinta y cuatro	35	34	24
veintiuno	21	31	28
treinta y tres	31	23	33
treinta	33	20	30
veintidós	22	20	28

52. How Much?

Write the Spanish words that match the price of each item.
Use the word bank to help you spell.

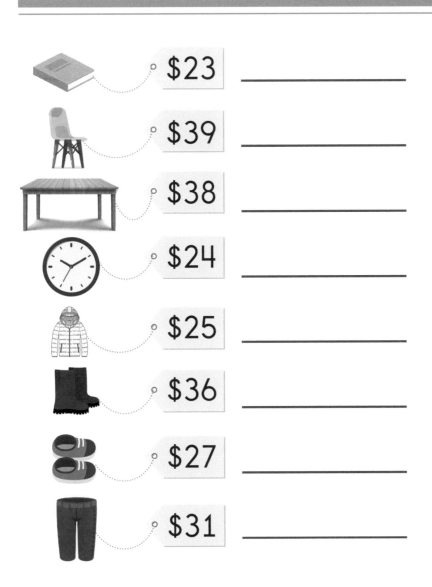

$23 _____

$39 _____

$38 _____

$24 _____

$25 _____

$36 _____

$27 _____

$31 _____

WORD BANK

• veintitrés • treinta y uno • veinticuatro • treinta y nueve • veinticinco
• veintisiete • treinta y ocho • treinta y seis

53. Being Polite

Say the Spanish words. Then trace the words.

Gracias / Thank you	De nada / You're welcome
[GRAH-see-ahs]	[DEH NAH-dah]

Gracias   Gracias

De nada   De nada

54. Introductions and Greetings

Say the Spanish words. Then trace the words.

¿Cómo te llamas? / What is your name? [KOH-moh teh YAH-mahs]	Me llamo . . . / My name is . . . [meh YAH-moh]

¿Cómo estás? / How are you? [KOH-moh ehs-TAHS]	Estoy bien / I'm fine [ehs-TOH-eeh bee-ehn]

¿Cómo te llamas?   ¿Cómo te llamas?

Me llamo   Me llamo

¿Cómo estás?   ¿Cómo estás?

Estoy bien   Estoy bien

55. Which Expression?

Use the word bank to write the responses.

1. Gracias

   _____

2. ¿Cómo estás?

   _____

3. Cómo te llamas?

   _____

Now fill in the blanks. Use the word bank to help you spell.

1. ¿C__m__ t__ l__a__ __s?

2. __ r __ c i __ s

3. ¿__ó __o e__t __s?

WORD BANK

- Me llamo ● De nada ● Estoy bien ● Gracias
- ¿Cómo estás? ● ¿Cómo te llamas?

56. Translate the Expression

Write the expressions in Spanish.

1. I'm fine.

_____

2. What's your name?

_____

3. How are you?

_____

4. You're welcome.

_____

5. My name is . . .

_____

6. Thank you.

_____

57. Food Fun

Say the words. Then trace the words.

EHL oo-EH-voh **EGG**

el huevo el huevo

EHL PLAH-tah-noh **BANANA**

el plátano el plátano

LAH mahn-SAH-nah **APPLE**

la manzana la manzana

LAHS OO-vahs **GRAPES**

las uvas las uvas

LAH SOH-pah **SOUP**

la sopa la sopa

EHL KEH-soh **CHEESE**

el queso el queso

EHL PAHN **BREAD**

el pan el pan

EHL POH-yoh **CHICKEN**

el pollo el pollo

58. Which Food?

Say the words. Then circle the matching picture.

el pollo

el pan

el queso

la sopa

las uvas

la manzana

el plátano

el huevo

59. Food Mix

Draw a line from each picture to the matching words.

las uvas

la manzana

el queso

el plátano

el huevo

el pan

la sopa

el pollo

60. Guess the Food

Write the answer to each clue in Spanish.
Use the word bank to help you spell.

1. This food is liquid and is served in a bowl. _____

2. This food grows on a vine and comes in a bunch. _____

3. Monkeys like this food after peeling it _____

4. This food is used to make toast _____

5. This food can be melted. _____

6. Hens lay this food. _____

7. This food is a meat. _____

8. This food grows on a tree and is usually red. _____

WORD BANK

- la sopa - el huevo - la manzana - el queso - el pollo
- el plátano - las uvas - el pan

61. In the Refrigerator

Draw and color the foods.
Use the word bank to say the words as you draw.

WORD BANK

- la sopa
- el huevo
- la manzana
- el queso
- el pollo
- el plátano
- las uvas
- el pan

62. What Doesn't Belong?

Write the food that is different from the other foods on each shelf. Use the word bank to help you spell.

WORD BANK

- la sopa
- el huevo
- la manzana
- el queso
- el pollo
- el plátano
- las uvas
- el pan

63. Say and Trace Family

Say the Spanish words. Then trace the words.

la mamá / mom	el papá / dad
[LAH mah-MAH]	[EHL pah-PAH]

la hermana / sister	el hermano / brother
[LAH ehr-MAH-nah]	[EHL ehr-MAH-noh]

la mamá   la mamá

el papá   el papá

la hermana   la hermana

el hermano   el hermano

64. Family Time

Say the Spanish words. Then trace the words.

el abuelo / grandpa

[EHL ah-boo-EH-loh]

la abuela / grandma

[LAH ah-boo-EH-lah]

la tía / aunt

[LAH TEE-ah]

el tío / uncle

[EHL TEE-oh]

el abuelo   el abuelo

la abula   la abula

la tia   la tía

el tío   el tío

65. Scrambled Family

Unscramble the words. Say each word as you write it.

le íto _____

el noremah _____

al labuae _____

le apáp _____

la aít _____

al remanha _____

el boalue _____

al ámma _____

66. All in the Family

Use the word bank to complete each sentence.

1. My dad's mother is my_____.

2. My mom's sister is my_____.

3. My mom's brother is my_____.

4. My dad's father is my_____.

5. My dad is my uncle's_____.

6. My mom is my aunt's_____.

7. My parents are my_____.
   and my _____.

WORD BANK

mamá • papá • abuela • abuelo • hermano • hermana • tía • tío

67. Family Match

Draw a line from the Spanish words to
the matching English words.

la mamá   aunt

el papá   sister

la hermana   uncle

el hermano   grandpa

el abuelo   father

la abuela   mother

la tía   brother

el tío   grandma

68. Who Is It?

How is everyone related to José?
Use Spanish words to complete the sentences.

Paco

Sofía

Verónica

María

Mateo

Diego

José

Paloma

1. Paco is José's _____.

2. Verónica is José's _____.

3. Paloma is José's _____.

4. Sofía is José's _____.

5. Mateo is José's _____.

6. Diego is José's _____.

7. María is José's _____.

69. Classroom Objects

Say the words. Then trace the words.

LAH PLOO-MAH **PEN**

la pluma

la pluma

EHL LAH-pees **PENCIL**

el lápiz

el lápiz

EHL ehs-kree-TOHR-eeh-oh **DESK**

el escritorio

el escritorio

LAH SEE-yah **CHAIR**

la silla

la silla

EHL boh-rrah-DOHR **ERASER**

el borrador

el borrador

LAH REH-glah **RULER**

la regla

la regla

70. More Classroom Objects

Say the words. Then trace the words.

LAH MEH-SAH **TABLE**

la mesa   la mesa

EHL LEE-broh **BOOK**

el libro   el libro

LAHS tee-HEH-rahs **SCISSORS**

las tijeras   las tijeras

EHL reh-LOH **CLOCK**

el reloj   el reloj

LAH moh-CHEE-lah **BACKPACK**

la mochila   la mochila

EHL pah-PEHL **PAPER**

el papel   el papel

71. Classroom Match

Draw a line from each picture to the matching words.

la pluma

el lápiz

el escritorio

la silla

el borrador

la regla

72. More Matching

Draw a line from each picture to the matching words.

el libro

las tijeras

el reloj

la mochila

el papel

la mesa

73. Color the Classroom

Say the words. Then draw and color a picture of each object.

el papel	el lápiz
el libro	el escritorio
el reloj	la silla

74. More Coloring

Say the words. Then draw and color a picture of each object.

el borrador	la pluma
la mesa	las tijeras
la regla	la mochila

75. Say and Trace Directions

Say the Spanish words. Then trace the words.

AH-RREE-BAH **UP**

arriba   arriba

ah-BAH-hoh **DOWN**

abajo   abajo

ees-kee-EHR-dah **LEFT**

izquierda   izquierda

deh-REH-chah **RIGHT**

derecha   derecha

ehn-SEE-mah **OVER**

encima   encima

deh-BAH-hoh **UNDER**

debajo   debajo

ah-foo-EH-rah **OUTSIDE**

afuera   afuera

ah-DEHN-troh **INSIDE**

adentro   adentro

76. Match the Directions

Draw a line from each picture to the matching word.

izquierda
afuera
abajo
debajo
derecha
encima
adentro
arriba

77. Where Is the Butterfly?

Write the location of the butterfly in relation to its cage. Use the word bank to help you spell.

_____   _____   _____

_____   _____   _____

WORD BANK

○ izquierda ○ afuera ○ debajo ○ derecha ○ encima ○ adentro

78. Draw the Directions

Follow the instructions to draw the pictures.

1. Draw a child throwing a ball *arriba*.

2. Draw a ball to the *izquierda* of the child.

3. Draw a ball *encima* the child.

4. Draw a ball *debajo* the child.

5. Draw the child with the ball *afuera* a house.

6. Draw the child with the ball *adentro* a house.

arriba	izquierda	encima
debajo	afuera	adentro

79. Say and Trace the Feelings

Say the Spanish words. Then trace the words.

FEH-LEES **HAPPY**

feliz   feliz

TREES-teh **SAD**

triste   triste

ah-soos-TAH-doh **SCARED**

asustado   asustado

eh-noh-HAH-doh **MAD**

enojado   enojado

kahn-SAH-doh **TIRED**

cansado   cansado

ah-boo-RREE-doh **BORED**

aburrido   aburrido

80. Match the Feelings

Draw a line from each picture to the matching word.

triste

| feliz |

| cansado |

| asustado |

| aburrido |

| enojado |

81. How Do You Feel?

Write the answer to each question.
Use the word bank to help you spell.

1. How do you feel when you don't get enough sleep?

   _____

2. How do you feel when you open great gifts on your birthday?_____

3. How do you feel when you have nothing to do?

   _____

4. How do you feel when you are in bed and hear a loud, strange noise?_____

5. How do you feel when somebody takes your favorite toy without asking?_____

6. How do you feel when your best friend moves far away?_____

WORD BANK

● triste ● feliz ● cansado ● asustado ● aburrido ● enojado

82. Which Feeling?

Circle the word that
matches each picture.

1. triste, feliz, cansado

2. asustado, aburrido, enojado

3. feliz, triste, cansado

4. aburrido, asustado, feliz

5. triste, cansado, asustado

6. enojado, feliz, aburrido

83. Draw the Feeling

Draw the children's faces to match their emotions.

1. triste

2. cansado

3. asustado

4. enojado

5. feliz

84. Mixed-Up Feelings

Unscramble the words and write them in Spanish.
Then write the words in English.

1. jonedoa _____

2. sondaca _____

3. lezif _____

4. satoduas _____

5. dariboru _____

6. tesrit _____

85. The Seasons

Say the Spanish words.
Then trace the words.

el invierno / winter

[EHL een-vee-EHR-noh]

la primavera / spring

[LAH pree-mah-VEH-rah]

el verano / summer

[EHL veh-RAH-noh]

el otoño / autumn

[EHL oh-TOH-nyoh]

el invierno   el invierno

la primavera   la primavera

el verano   el verano

el otoño   el otoño

86. Which Season?

Write the answer to each question. Use the word bank to help you spell.

1. In which season do the leaves fall? _____

2. In which season is it cold? _____

3. In which season is it hot? _____

4. In which season do the flowers start
   to bloom? _____

WORD BANK

• en el verano • en la primavera • en el invierno • en el otoño

87. Weather Words

Say the Spanish words. Then trace the words.

LAH YOO-VEE-AH **THE RAIN**

la lluvia   la lluvia

LAH nee-EH-veh **THE SNOW**

la nieve   la nieve

EHL kah-LOHR **THE HEAT**

el calor   el calor

EHL FREE-oh **THE COLD**

el frío   el frío

EHL vee-EHN-toh **THE WIND**

el viento   el viento

LAS NOO-behs **THE CLOUDS**

las nubes   las nubes

88. Weather Matching

Draw a line from each picture to the matching words.

| el calor |
| el viento |
| el frío |
| las nubes |
| la lluvia |
| la nieve |

89. Which Word?

Use the word bank to complete each sentence.

1. If you need an umbrella, it is because of _____.

2. If it is 100 degrees outside, people talk about _____ _____.

3. If it is 5 degrees outside, people talk about_____.

4. You can build a snowman if there is _____.

5. Rain comes from _____.

6. If you are outside and your hat blows off, it is because of_____.

WORD BANK

las nubes • el calor • la lluvia • el viento • la nieve • el frío

90. Draw the Weather

Follow the instructions to draw the pictures.

1. Draw a person under *las nubes*.

2. Draw a tree in *el viento*.

3. Draw your house in *el invierno*.

4. Draw a flower in *la lluvia*.

5. Draw a snake in *el calor* of the desert.

6. Draw your house in *la primavera*.

1	2	3

4	5	6

91. A or Some

All nouns in Spanish are either **masculine** or **feminine**.
If the Spanish noun is **masculine** and **singular**, use *un*. If it's
masculine and **plural**, use *unos*. If it's **feminine** and
singular, use *una*. If it's **feminine** and **plural**, use *unas*.
Say the Spanish words. Then trace the words.

un libro / a book	unos libros / some books
[OON LEE-broh]	[OO-nohs LEE-brohs]

una uva / a grape	unas uvas / some grapes
[OO-nah OOH-vah]	[OO-nahs OOH-vahs]
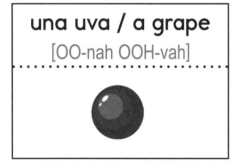	

un libro   un libro

unos libros   unos libros

una uva   una uva

unas uvas   unas uvas

92. Change to Plural

Write the plurals in Spanish.

un libro

una uva

una silla

un huevo

una mesa

un tío

93. Write the Words

Write the Spanish words that match each picture.

❄ _____

▬ _____

🧀 _____

👩 _____

40 _____

🍎 _____

FALL _____

30 _____

94. Draw the Sentence

Draw a picture of each sentence or phrase.

1. El papel está debajo del escritorio.

2. El hermano está asustado.

3. El huevo está encima de la mesa.

4. El abuelo está feliz.

5. veintidós uvas

6. Hay unos plátanos bajo la lluvia.

1	2	3

4	5	6

95. Family Pictures

Draw a picture of each sentence.

1. Draw *un papá* eating *la sopa* and looking *enojado.*

2. Draw *un tío* to the *derecha* of *una mochila.*

3. Draw *una mamá* eating *el pan afuera.*

4. Draw *unas tijeras* to the *izquierda* of *un libro* on *una mesa.*

5. Draw *una tía* eating *un plátano* in *el viento.*

6. Draw *una abuela* eating *el pollo* and looking *cansada.*

1	2	3

4	5	6

96. Translate It

Translate the following words and phrases from English to Spanish.

1. What's your name? _____

2. The winter _____

3. How are you? _____

4. Above _____

5. I'm fine. _____

6. The heat _____

7. You're welcome. _____

8. The cold _____

9. My name is _____

10. Bored _____

11. The spring _____

12. Thank you. _____

Grade 3

97. Ways to Say "You"

The pronoun **"you"** (when talking to one person, singular) has two different forms in Spanish: **tú** and **usted**. Read the differences between them. Then write the word at the bottom.

Tú

1. Someone you refer to using their first name.

2. Your sister, brother, or cousin.

3. A close friend.

4. A classmate or teammate.

_____

Usted

1. An older person.

2. Somebody you do not know.

3. Someone with a title, like Ms., Mr., or Dr.

4. When you are unsure, use **Usted.**

_____

98. Which You?

Write Tú or Usted to address each person.

1. Your brother _____

2. Your teacher _____

3. Another child you just met _____

4. An adult you just met _____

5. A police officer _____

6. Your friend _____

7. Your doctor _____

8. Your pet _____

99. Describe the Car

Say each Spanish word. Then write the Spanish word to match each picture.

viejo / old [vee-EH-hoh]	nuevo / new [noo-EH-voh]

_____

_____

grande / big [GRAHN-deh]	pequeño / little [peh-KEH-nyoh]

_____

_____

100. Feminine and Masculine

In Spanish, nouns and adjectives are either **masculine** or **feminine**. If a noun is **masculine**, its adjective must also be masculine. For example, "El abuel**o** es viej**o**." If a noun is **feminine**, its adjective must also be feminine. For example, "La abuel**a** es viej**a**."

Write the following adjectives in both the masculine and feminine forms.

bueno [boo-EH-noh] / good _____

malo [MAH-loh] / bad _____

divertido [dee-vehr-TEE-doh] / fun _____

delicioso [deh-lee-see-OH-soh] / delicious _____

alto [AHL-toh] / tall _____

bajo [BAH-hoh] / short _____

101. Match the Words

Draw a line from each Spanish word to the matching English word.

bueno	short
pequeño	good
malo	old
bajo	small
divertido	bad
alto	delicious
viejo	fun
delicioso	tall

102. Which Word?

Use the word bank to complete each sentence.

1. The baby is young, but the 100-year-old man is

   _____.

2. The pond is small, but the ocean is _____.

3. The dry cake isn't good, but the fresh bread is

   _____.

4. The basketball player is very tall, but his young child is

   _____.

5. Sitting alone in my room can be boring, but going to the pool is _____.

6. The elephant is big, but the mouse is _____.

7. Sharing is kind, but stealing is _____.

8. The song I've heard many times is old, but the song I just heard for the first time is _____.

WORD BANK

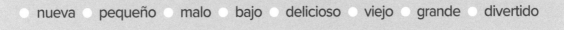

nueva ● pequeño ● malo ● bajo ● delicioso ● viejo ● grande ● divertido

103. Food Fun

Say the Spanish words.
Then write the words in Spanish.

el postre / dessert
[EHL POHS-treh]

el helado / ice cream
[EHL eh-LAH-doh]

la galleta / cookie
[LAH gah-YEH-tah]

el pastel / cake
[EHL pahs-TEHL]

104. Writing Food

Say the Spanish words.
Then write the words in Spanish.

---

la bebida / drink
[LAH beh-BEE-dah]

_____

la leche / milk
[LAH LEH-cheh]

_____

el jugo / juice
[EHL HOO-goh]

_____

el agua / water
[EHL AH-goo-ah]

_____

105. It Doesn't Belong

Write the food or drink that does not belong in each row.

106. Guess the Word

Write the Spanish word for the drink or food that matches each sentence.

1. It's clear and has no taste. _____

2. It's white and cows make it. _____

3. Fruits can be made into it. _____

4. It's cold and comes in many flavors. _____

5. You put candles on it for your birthday. _____

6. Cookies, cake, ice cream, and candy bars are all examples of this. _____

107. Color It Up

Follow the directions to color the picture.

1. Color *el jugo anaranjado.*

2. Color *el agua azul.*

3. Color *la galleta color café.*

4. Color *el pastel amarillo.*

5. Color *la leche blanca.*

6. Color *la bebida verde.*

108. Your Favorites

Write the answer to each question.
Answer in Spanish if you can.

1. What is your favorite *comida*? _____

2. What is your favorite *bebida*? _____

3. What is your favorite *jugo*? _____

4. What is your favorite *postre*? _____

5. What is your favorite kind of *pastel*? _____

6. What is your favorite kind of *galleta*? _____

109. Writing at Home

Say the Spanish words.
Then write the words in Spanish.

la casa / house [LAH KAH-sah]	la puerta / door [LAH poo-EHR-tah]	la ventana / window [LAH vehn-TAH-nah]

la cocina / kitchen [LAH koh-SEE-nah]	la estufa / stove [LAH ehs-TOO-fah]	el tenedor / fork [EHL teh-neh-DOHR]

el cuchillo / knife [EHL koo-CHEE-yoh]	la cuchara / spoon [LAH koo-CHAH-rah]	el vaso / glass [EHL VAH-soh]

110. More Writing at Home

Say the Spanish words.
Then write words in Spanish.

el dormitorio / bedroom
[EHL dohr-mee-TOH-ree-oh]

la cama / bed
[LAH KAH-mah]

la almohada / pillow
[LAH ahl-moh-AH-dah]

la manta / blanket
[LAH MAHN-tah]

la lámpara / lamp
[LAH LAHM-pah-rah]

el baño / bathroom
[EHL BAH-nyoh]

la ducha / shower
[LAH DOO-chah]

la toalla / towel
[LAH toh-AH-yah]

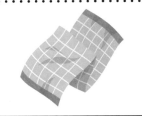

el jabón / soap
[EHL hah-BOHN]

111. Home Matching

Draw a line from each picture to the matching words.
Then say the words.

el tenedor

la puerta

la toalla

la cama

la cuchara

el dormitorio

la ducha

el jabón

GRADE 3: AT HOME

112. Scrambled House

Unscramble the words. Use the word bank to help you spell.

 1. al ralapám _____

 2. al taman _____

 **3.** le ridomitoor _____

 4. al domalaha _____

 5. al chuad _____

 6. le notdeer _____

7. al tafues _____

 8. al hacruca _____

WORD BANK

● la puerta ● la ventana ● la cocina ● la estufa ● el tenedor ● el cuchillo
● la cuchara ● el vaso ● el dormitorio ● la cama ● la almohada
● la manta ● el baño ● la toalla ● la lámpara ● la ducha ● el jabón

113. Guess the Word

Write the Spanish word that matches each sentence.
Use the word bank to help you spell.

1. You use this to cut food. _____

2. You use this to eat soup. _____

3. You drink out of this. _____

4. You put your head on this. _____

5. You sleep on this. _____

6. You look through this to see outside. _____

7. You go through this to get in and out of your house.

   _____

8. People live in this. _____

9. You brush your teeth in this room. _____

10. You clean your body with this. _____

WORD BANK

- la puerta
- la ventana
- la casa
- el cuchillo
- la cuchara
- el vaso
- la cama
- la almohada
- el baño
- el jabón

114. Home Sweet Home

Draw the inside of your home. Use the word bank to label 10 things in your home. Then color your picture.

WORD BANK

- la puerta
- la ventana
- la cocina
- la estufa
- el tenedor
- el cuchillo
- la cuchara
- el vaso
- el dormitorio
- la cama
- la almohada
- la manta
- la lámpara
- el baño
- la ducha
- la toalla
- el jabón

115. Writing the Neighborhood

Say the Spanish words. Then write the words in Spanish.

la calle / street	el auto / car	la biblioteca / library	la escuela / school
[LAH KAH-yeh]	[EHL AH-ooh-toh]	[LAH bee-blee-oh-TEH-kah]	[LAH ehs-koo-EH-lah]
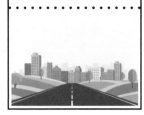			

_____   _____   _____   _____

el mercado / grocery store	el parque / park	el cine / the movie theater	el museo / the museum
[EHL mehr-KAH-doh]	[EHL PAHR-keh]	[EHL SEE-neh]	[EHL moo-SEH-oh]
		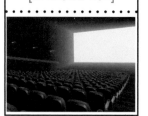	

_____   _____   _____   _____

116. Which Picture?

Say the words. Then circle the picture that matches the word.

la escuela

el parque

el auto

el museo

la biblioteca

el cine

la calle

el mercado

117. Missing Letters

Write the missing letters to complete the words.
Use the word bank to help you spell.

1. E__ au__ __ es n__e__o.

2. __a e__ __u__la es di__er__i__a.

3. El p__rqu__ es b__en__.

4. __l m__ __c__d__ es g__an__ __.

5. L__ c__l__e es g__i__.

6. La b__b__i__t__c__ es v__e__a.

7. El __u__eo es pe__u__ñ__.

WORD BANK

- la escuela
- el auto
- divertida
- grande
- el parque
- nuevo
- el mercado
- bueno
- pequeño
- es
- la calle
- vieja
- gris
- la biblioteca
- el museo

118. Neighborhood Picture

Draw a neighborhood. Use the word bank to label 8 things in the neighborhood. Then color your picture.

WORD BANK

- la calle
- la biblioteca
- el mercado
- el museo
- el cine
- el parque
- el auto
- la escuela

119. Guess the Word

Use the word bank to complete each sentence.

1. You can have a picnic at _____.

2. You learn from teachers at _____.

3. You borrow books at _____.

4. You buy food at _____.

5. You watch a movie at _____.

6. _____ drives on the street.

7. The car drives on _____.

8. At _____ you may see dinosaur bones.

WORD BANK

• la calle • la biblioteca • el mercado • el museo • el cine • el parque • el auto • la escuela

120. Translate the Neighborhood

Translate the sentences from English to Spanish. The word for "is" in Spanish is **es**. Remember that the adjective must be **feminine** or **masculine** to agree with the noun.

1. The street is bad. _____

2. The museum is fun. _____

3. The school is good. _____

4. The car is pink. _____

5. The movie theater is new. _____

6. The park is old. _____

7. The library is red. _____

8. The grocery store is small. _____

121. Write It Out

Say the Spanish words.
Then write the words in Spanish.

el fútbol / soccer	el fútbol americano / football	el baloncesto / basketball	la natación / swimming
[EHL FOOT-bohl]	[EHL FOOT-bohl ah-mehr-eeh-KAH-noh]	[EHL bah-lohn- SEHS-toh]	[LAH nah-tah- see-OHN]

_____ _____

el béisbol / baseball	el baile / dance	la lectura / reading	la música / music
[EHL BEH-ees-bohl]	[EHL BAH-ee-leh]	[LAH lehk-TOO-rah]	[LAH MOO-see-kah]

_____ _____

122. Draw It

Draw a sport or hobby from the word bank in each box.
Label each picture with the Spanish words.

WORD BANK

- el fútbol
- el fútbol americano
- el baloncesto
- la natación
- el béisbol
- el baile
- la lectura
- la música

123. Finish the Sentences

Use the word bank to complete each sentence.

1. You can strike out in _____.

2. There must be music if you want to enjoy _____.

3. You must be in the water if you want to participate in _____.

4. If you like _____ then you may want to visit *la biblioteca*.

5. When playing _____, only the goalkeepers can use their hands.

6. In _____, players must wear helmets.

7. In _____, the players must bounce or dribble the ball with one hand while moving both feet.

8. You can listen to _____ when you turn on the radio.

WORD BANK

- el fútbol
- el fútbol americano
- el baloncesto
- la natación
- el béisbol
- el baile
- la lectura
- la música

124. Drawing Fun

Say the words. Then draw pictures to match the words.

el béisbol

el fútbol

el baile

el fútbol americano

la lectura

el baloncesto

la música

la natación

125. Fix the Mistake

Rewrite the sentences to correct the underlined mistakes.
Use the word bank to help you spell.

1. El <u>balooncesto</u> es <u>buena</u>. _____

2. La <u>natassioón</u> es <u>divertido</u>. _____

3. El <u>baseball</u> es <u>nueva</u>. _____

4. El <u>footboól</u> es <u>vieja</u>. _____

5. El baile no es <u>mala</u>. _____

6. <u>El moosika</u> es grande. _____

WORD BANK

- fútbol
- bueno
- baloncesto
- natación
- malo
- béisbol
- viejo
- nuevo
- divertida
- la música

126. My Favorite Things

Answer questions 1 and 2 in Spanish.
Then answer questions 3 to 6 in English.

1. What is a sport you like to play?

   _____

2. What is a sport you like to watch?

   _____

3. What type of *música* do you like?

   _____

4. When you are enjoying *la lectura*, what books do you prefer? _____

5. What style of *baile* do you like best?

   _____

6. Do you prefer *la natación* inside or outside?

   _____

127. Write about People

Say the Spanish words. Then write the words in Spanish.

la maestra / teacher	el policía / police officer	el bombero / firefighter
[LAH-mah-EHS-trah]	[EHL poh-leeh-SEE-ah]	[EHL bohm-BEH-roh]

el médico / doctor	la enfermera / nurse	el veterinario / veterinarian
[EHL MEH-dee-koh]	[LAH ehn-fehr-MEH-rah]	[EHL veh-teh-ree-NAH-ree-oh]

128. Picture This

Say the words. Then circle the picture that matches the words.

el veterinario

el médico

el policía

la enfermera

la maestra

el bombero

129. Draw the Workers

Pick 4 workers from the word bank.
Draw and label a picture of each worker.
Then write a sentence describing each worker.

WORD BANK

- el veterinario
- el médico
- la maestra
- la enfermera
- el bombero
- el policía
- bajo
- alto
- viejo
- pequeño
- nuevo
- bueno
- malo
- divertido
- grande

130. Mixed-Up Workers

Unscramble the words.

le comdié _____

al traseam _____

le moorbeb _____

le nerativiore _____

al armeenerf _____

el cailoíp _____

131. Different Places

Say the Spanish words. Then write the words in Spanish.

el avión / airplane	el aeropuerto / airport	el tren / train	el autobús / bus
[EHL ah-vee-OHN]	[EHL ah-eh-roh-poo-HER-toh]	[EHL TREHN]	[EHL ah-oo-toh-BOOS]

_____ _____ _____ _____

la playa / beach	la montaña / mountain	la ciudad / city	el lago / lake
[LAH PLAH-yah]	[LAH mohn-TAH-nyah]	[LAH see-oo-DAHD]	[EHL LAH-goh]

 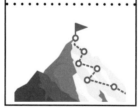  

_____ _____ _____ _____

132. Circling Places

Circle the picture that matches the words.

el lago

la montaña

la ciudad

la playa

el tren

el aeropuerto

el autobús

el avión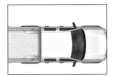

133. Around Town

Say the words. Then write the Spanish words.

la montaña _____

la playa _____

el tren _____

el lago _____

la ciudad _____

el autobús _____

el avión _____

el aeropuerto _____

134. Missing Letters

Fill in the missing letters. Use the word bank to help you spell.

1. El l__g__ es a__u__.

2. __a m__n__añ__ es a__t__.

3. L__ c__u__a__ es g__ __n__e.

4. L__ pl__y__ es b__e__a.

5. __l t__ __n es r__j__.

6. El ae__o__u__rt__ es d__v__r__i__o.

7. E__ a__ __o__ú__ es m__l__.

8. El av__ó__ es p__q__ __ñ__.

WORD BANK

- malo • bueno • la montaña • pequeño • grande • azul
- la playa • el tren • el lago • rojo • la ciudad • el autobús
- divertido • el avión • alta • el aeropuerto

135. Guess the Place

Use the word bank to complete each sentence.

1. I go to _____ to fly somewhere.

2. I go to the bus station to take _____.

3. There are many buildings and neighborhoods in _____.

4. One day, I will climb _____ to reach the summit.

5. On a hot day, I like to go swimming at _____.

6. I fly on _____ to travel faster.

7. I like to travel on _____ as it moves on the tracks.

8. I can go to _____ if I want to go fishing.

WORD BANK

el lago • la montaña • la ciudad • la playa • el tren
el aeropuerto • el autobús • el avión

136. Drawing Places

Pick 4 places from the word bank. Draw and label a picture of each place. Then write a sentence about each picture.

WORD BANK

● el lago   ● la montaña   ● la ciudad   ● la playa   ● el tren
● el aeropuerto   ● el autobús   ● el avión

137. Write the Actions

Say the Spanish words. Then write words in Spanish.

ir / go [eer]	caminar / walk [kah-mee-NAHR]	correr / run [koh-RREHR]
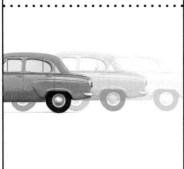		

_____   _____   _____

jugar / play [hoo-GAHR]	gustar / like [goos-TAHR]

_____   _____

138. More Actions

Say the Spanish words. Then write the words in Spanish.

no gustar / dislike	hablar / talk	comer / eat
[noh goos-TAHR]	[ah-BLAHR]	[koh-MERH]

_____ _____ _____

dormir / sleep	nadar / swim
[dohr-MEER]	[nah-DAHR]

_____ _____

139. Match the Actions

Draw a line from each English verb to the matching Spanish verb.

nadar	go
jugar	walk
gustar	run
comer	play
dormir	like
caminar	dislike
no gustar	talk
hablar	eat
ir	sleep
correr	swim

140. Guess the Word

Use the word bank to complete each sentence.

1. When it's hot outside, I like _____ in the water at the pool.

2. He is very quiet. He does not want _____.

3. It's difficult _____ at night if there's a lot of noise.

4. Because the school is near my house, I'd rather _____ than ride the bus.

5. She thinks broccoli is bad and doesn't like _____ it.

6. The friends _____ to dance. They think it's boring.

7. My uncle is going _____ to the store because he's in a hurry.

8. Her brother loves _____ baseball.

9. His grandparents like _____ on a trip every summer.

10. Most people _____ eating ice cream.

WORD BANK

● dormir ● caminar ● jugar ● comer ● no gustar ● hablar
nadar ● gustar ● ir ● correr

141. Draw the Sentences

Draw pictures to match each sentence.
Then write the sentences.

1. Al médico no le gusta nadar.

2. A la maestra le gusta correr.

3. La enfermera come el helado.

4. Al bombero le gusta jugar fútbol.

5. Al policía le gusta la lectura en la biblioteca.

6. El veterinario usa el jabón en el baño.

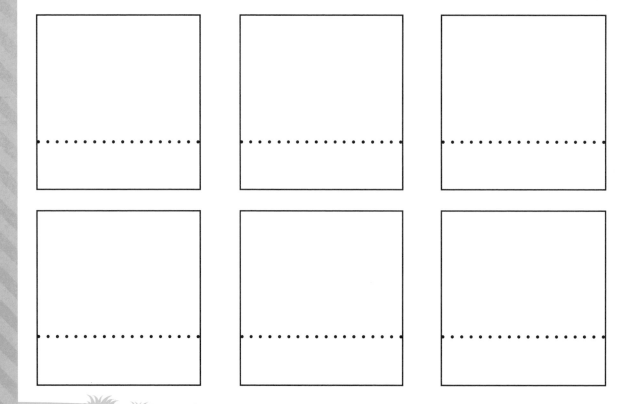

142. Translate It

Rewrite the sentences in Spanish.
Use the word bank to help you spell.

1. The museum is old. _____

2. The pillow is new. _____

3. The cake is delicious. _____

4. Talking is good. _____

5. Playing baseball is fun. _____

6. The mountain is tall. _____

7. The teacher is short. _____

8. The lake is small. _____

9. The airplane is big. _____

10. The park is bad. _____

WORD BANK

es • hablar • el parque • el lago • viejo • alta • bueno • el museo

la almohada • pequeño • el avión • jugar • nueva

el pastel • el béisbol • divertido • delicioso • la montaña

baja • la maestra • malo • grande

143. Missing Letters

Fill in the blanks to complete the Spanish sentences.
Use the word bank to help you spell.

1. El cu__hi__l__ está en l__ c__c__n__.

2. __a __i__d__d es g__a__d__.

3. La __u__ __ a está en __l ba__o.

4. T__ e__es __i he__ma__a.

5. U__t__d __s m__ m__d__ __o.

6. La e__t__f__ está bu__n__.

7. __a __an__a e__tá en e__ d__r__i__o__io.

8. El b__ __le es __iv__r__id__.

9. Me __u__ta i__ a la __la__a para __ad__r.

10. __l p__s__r__ está en e__ m__r__a__o.

WORD BANK

- en la cocina - ir - médico grande - en el baño - eres - el cuchillo
- la ciudad - tú divertido - mi - el postre - hermana - es - usted
- médico - a la playa - la ducha - para nadar - en el dormitorio
- la manta - el baile - la estufa - me gusta - la ducha - buena
- en el mercado - está

144. Draw It

Write 6 sentences in Spanish using at least three words from Grade 3. Draw a picture of each sentence.

ANSWER KEY

GRADE 1

EXERCISE 1

1. uno
2. dos
3. tres
4. cuatro
5. cinco
6. seis
7. siete
8. ocho
9. nueve
10. diez

EXERCISE 2

11. once
12. doce
13. trece
14. catorce
15. quince
16. dieciséis
17. diecisiete
18. dieciocho
19. diecinueve
20. veinte

EXERCISE 3

1. 6
2. 4
3. 3
4. 2
5. 5
6. 1

EXERCISE 4

catorce - 14
doce - 12
quince - 15
veinte - 20
diecisiete - 17
once - 11
dieciocho -18
trece - 13
dieciséis- 16
diecinueve -19

EXERCISE 5

Answers will vary.

EXERCISE 6

Answers will vary.

EXERCISE 7

dos
cuatro
seis
ocho
diez

EXERCISE 8

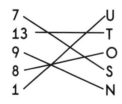

7   U
13 ————— T
9   O
8   S
1   N

EXERCISE 9

lunes
martes
miércoles
jueves
viernes
sábado
domingo

EXERCISE 10

martes
jueves
sábado
lunes
miércoles
viernes
domingo

EXERCISE 11

1. sábado
2. lunes
3. jueves
4. martes
5. miércoles
6. domingo
7. viernes

EXERCISE 12

1. domingo
2. martes
3. lunes
4. sábado
5. viernes
6. miércoles
7. jueves

EXERCISE 13

enero
febrero
marzo
abril
mayo
junio
julio
agosto
septiembre
octubre
noviembre
diciembre

EXERCISE 14

1. junio
2. marzo
3. abril
4. mayo
5. enero
6. febrero

EXERCISE 15

1. noviembre
2. diciembre
3. septiembre
4. agosto
5. julio
6. octubre

EXERCISE 16

diciembre
junio
octubre
febrero
agosto
septiembre
mayo
julio
enero
marzo
noviembre
abril

EXERCISE 17

Answers will vary.

EXERCISE 18

Answers will vary.

EXERCISE 19

An image of a purple flower
An image of a blue flower
An image of a yellow flower
An image of a red flower
An image of a pink flower
An image of an orange flower

EXERCISE 20

An image of a black shirt
An image of a white shirt
An image of a gray shirt
An image of a green shirt
An image of a brown shirt

EXERCISE 21

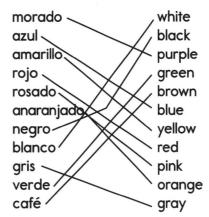

morado — purple
azul — blue
amarillo — yellow
rojo — red
rosado — pink
anaranjado — orange
negro — black
blanco — white
gris — gray
verde — green
café — brown

EXERCISE 22

An image of a rainbow with the colors,
top to bottom:
orange
yellow
green
blue
red
purple

Hola
Adiós

Buenos días
Buenas tardes
Buenas noches

Hola — Hello
Adiós — Goodbye
Buenos días — Good morning
Buenas tardes — Good afternoon
Buenas noches — Good evening/night

Buenos días
Adiós
Buenas noches

El taco
Los tacos
La vaca
Las vacas

Las vacas
El taco
La vaca
Los tacos

la cara
los ojos
las orejas
la nariz
la boca
los dientes
el cabello

el hombro
el brazo
el codo
la mano
el dedo de la mano
la pierna
la rodilla
el estómago
el pie
el dedo del pie
el cuerpo

Image of a face with these labels:
la cara
los ojos
las orejas
la nariz
la boca
los dientes
el cabello

el hombro
el brazo
el codo
la mano
el dedo de la mano
la pierna
la rodilla
el estómago
el pie
el dedo del pie
el cuerpo

la camisa
la gorra
la chaqueta
la bufanda
el suéter
los guantes

EXERCISE 34

el vestido
los pantalones
el cinturón
los zapatos
los calcetines
las botas

EXERCISE 35

las botas

la chaqueta

los zapatos

los guantes

el cinturón

el suéter

EXERCISE 36

la gorra

la bufanda

la camisa

el vestido

los pantalones

los calcetines

EXERCISE 37

1. los guantes
2. los pantalones
3. el cinturón
4. la bufanda
5. los calcetines
6. la gorra

EXERCISE 38

Image of a body wearing a dress
Image of a body wearing a sweater
Image of a body wearing a jacket
Image of a body wearing a shirt
Image of a body wearing shoes
Image of a body wearing boots

EXERCISE 39

An image of a dog with *el perro* written
An image of a cat with *el gato* written
An image of a bird with *el pájaro* written
An image of a snake with *la serpiente* written
An image of a fish with *el pez* written
An image of a cow with *la vaca* written

EXERCISE 40

An image of a horse with *el caballo* written
An image of a lion with *el león* written
An image of a tiger with *el tigre* written
An image of a bear with *el oso* written
An image of a monkey with *el mono* written
An image of a frog with *la rana* written

EXERCISE 41

An image of a bee with *la abeja* written
An image of a duck with *el pato* written
An image of a turtle with *la tortuga* written
An image of a butterfly with *la mariposa* written
An image of an elephant with *el elefante* written
An image of a pig with *el cerdo* written

EXERCISE 42

el perro
el gato
el pájaro
la serpiente
el pez
la vaca

EXERCISE 43

1. La serpiente
2. El perro
3. El pez
4. El gato
5. El pájaro
6. La vaca

EXERCISE 44

la abeja written under an image of a bee
el pato written under an image of a duck
la tortuga written under an image of a turtle
la mariposa written under an image of a butterfly
el elefante written under an image of an elephant
el cerdo written under an image of a pig

EXERCISE 45

An image of 2 brown bears
An image of 10 blue butterflies
An image of 13 green snakes
An image of 8 orange fish
An image of 6 blue birds
An image of 3 yellow ducks

EXERCISE 46

1. martes; 2. la nariz; 3. enero; 4. los pies;
5. lunes; 6. la camisa; 7. sábado;
8. los dientes

EXERCISE 47

los pantalones
miércoles
el caballo
los ojos
Buenos días
la pierna
marzo
las orejas

ears
leg
Good morning
March
pants
Wednesday
horse
eyes

EXERCISE 48

1. viernes; 2. los guantes; 3. Buenas tardes;
4. la boca; 5. la rana; 6. jueves; 7. Buenas
noches; 8. los calcetines; 9. el estómago;
10. diciembre

GRADE 2

EXERCISE 49

veintiuno
veintidós
veintitrés
veinticuatro
veinticinco
veintiséis
veintisiete
veintiocho
veintinueve
treinta

EXERCISE 50

treinta y uno
treinta y dos
treinta y tres
treinta y cuatro
treinta y cinco
treinta y seis
treinta y siete
treinta y ocho
treinta y nueve
cuarenta

37
28
40
34
21
33
30
22

Image of a book with *veintitrés* next to it
An image of a chair with *treinta y nueve* next to it
An image of a table with *treinta y ocho* next to it
An image of a clock with *veinticuatro* next to it
An image of a jacket with *veinticinco* next to it
An image of boots with *treinta y seis* next to it
An image of shoes with *veintisiete* next to it
An image of pants with *treinta y uno* next to it

Gracias
De nada

¿Cómo te llamas?
Me llamo
¿Cómo estás?
Estoy bien

1.   De nada
2.   Estoy bien
3.   Me llamo
4.   ¿Cómo te llamas?
5.   Gracias
6.   ¿Cómo estás?

1.   Estoy bien
2.   ¿Cómo te llamas?
3.   ¿Cómo estás?
4.   De nada
5.   Me llamo
6.   Gracias

el huevo
el plátano
la manzana
las uvas
la sopa
el queso
el pan
el pollo

An image of a chicken leg
An image of a loaf of bread
An image of a piece of cheese
An image of a bowl of soup
An image of a bunch of grapes
An image of an apple
An image of a banana
An image of an egg

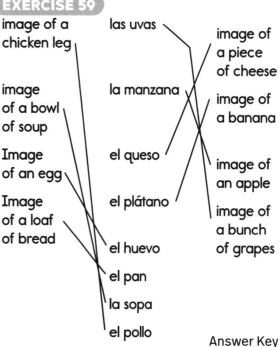

1. la sopa
2. las uvas
3. el plátano
4. el pan
5. el queso
6. el huevo
7. el pollo
8. la manzana

EXERCISE 61

An image of a refrigerator with images of an egg, a chicken leg, a piece of cheese, a loaf of bread, a banana, an apple, and a bowl of soup

EXERCISE 62

1. la sopa
2. el pan
3. el queso

EXERCISE 63

la mamá
el papá
la hermana
el hermano

EXERCISE 64

el abuelo
la abuela
la tía
el tío

EXERCISE 65

1. el tío
2. el hermano
3. la abuela
4. el papá
5. la tía
6. la hermana
7. el abuelo
8. la mamá

EXERCISE 66

1. abuela
2. tía
3. tío
4. abuelo
5. hermano
6. hermana
7. mamá and my papá

EXERCISE 67

la mamá — mother
el papá — father
la hermana — sister
el hermano — brother
el abuelo — grandpa
la abuela — grandma
la tía — aunt
el tío — uncle

EXERCISE 68

1. abuelo
2. tía
3. hermana
4. abuela
5. papá
6. tío
7. mamá

EXERCISE 69

la pluma
el lápiz
el escritorio
la silla
el borrador
la regla

EXERCISE 70

la mesa
el libro
las tijeras
el reloj
la mochila
el papel

EXERCISE 71

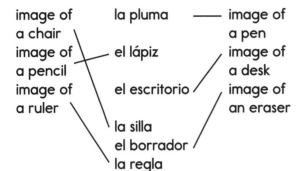

image of a chair	la pluma	image of a pen
image of a pencil	el lápiz	image of a desk
image of a ruler	el escritorio	image of an eraser
	la silla	
	el borrador	
	la regla	

EXERCISE 72

image of a clock	la mesa	image of a book
image of a table	el libro	image of scissors
image of a piece of paper	las tijeras	image of a backpack
	el reloj	
	la mochila	
	el papel	

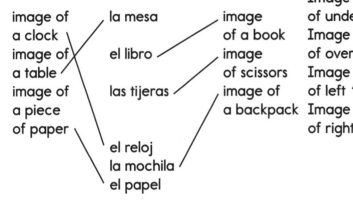

EXERCISE 73

An image of a piece of paper
An image of a pencil
An image of a book
An image of a desk
An image of a clock
An image of a chair

EXERCISE 74

An image of an eraser
An image of a pen
An image of a table
An image of scissors
An image of a ruler
An image of a backpack

EXERCISE 75

arriba
abajo
izquierda
derecha
encima
debajo
afuera
adentro

EXERCISE 76

Image of under	izquierda	image of outside
Image of over	afuera	image of inside
Image of left	abajo	image of up
Image of right	debajo	image of down
	derecha	
	encima	
	adentro	
	arriba	

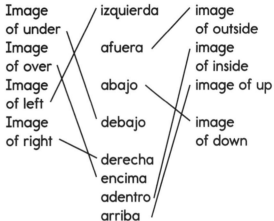

EXERCISE 77

1. derecha
2. debajo
3. izquierda
4. encima
5. adentro
6. afuera

EXERCISE 78

Image of a child throwing a ball up
Image of a ball to the left of a child
Image of a ball over the child
Image of a ball under the child
Image of a child with a ball outside a house
Image of a child with a ball inside a house

EXERCISE 79

feliz
triste
asustado
enojado
cansado
aburrido

EXERCISE 80

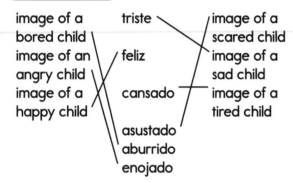

image of a bored child — triste
image of an angry child — feliz
image of a happy child — cansado
image of a scared child
image of a sad child — asustado
image of a tired child — aburrido
enojado

EXERCISE 81

1. cansado
2. feliz
3. aburrido
4. asustado
5. enojado
6. triste

EXERCISE 82

1. cansado
2. enojado
3. feliz
4. asustado
5. triste
6. aburrido

EXERCISE 83

Image of a child looking sad
Image of a child looking tired
Image of a child looking scared
Image of a child looking angry
Image of a child looking happy

EXERCISE 84

1. enojado
2. cansado
3. feliz
4. asustado
5. aburrido
6. triste

EXERCISE 85

el invierno
la primavera
el verano
el otoño

EXERCISE 86

1. el otoño
2. el invierno
3. el verano
4. la primavera

EXERCISE 87

la lluvia
la nieve
el calor
el frío
el viento
las nubes

EXERCISE 88

image of the wind — el calor — image of snow
image of the sun — el viento — image clouds
image of rain — el frío — image of the cold
las nubes
la lluvia
la nieve

1. la lluvia
2. el calor
3. el frío
4. la nieve
5. las nubes
6. el viento

An image of a person under clouds
An image of a tree in the wind
An image of a house in the winter
An image of a flower in the rain
An image of a snake in a hot desert
An image of a house in the spring

un libro
unos libros
una uva
unas uvas

1. unos libros
2. unas uvas
3. unas sillas
4. unos huevos
5. unas mesas
6. unos tíos

1. la nieve
2. el borrador
3. el queso
4. la abuela
5. cuarenta
6. la manzana
7. el otoño
8. treinta

1. Image of a piece of paper under desk
2. Image of a scared boy
3. An egg on the table
4. A happy grandpa
5. 22 grapes
6. Bananas in the rain

Image of an angry-looking dad eating soup
Image of an uncle to the right of
a backpack
Image of a mom eating bread outside
Image of scissors to the left of a book
on a table
Image of an aunt eating a banana in the wind
Image of a tired-looking grandma eating a
chicken leg

1. ¿Cómo te llamas?
2. el invierno
3. ¿Cómo estás?
4. arriba
5. Estoy bien.
6. el calor
7. De nada.
8. el frío
9. Me llamo
10. aburrido
11. la primavera
12. Gracias.

GRADE 3

Tú Usted

EXERCISE 98

1. Tú
2. Usted
3. Tú
4. Usted
5. Usted
6. Tú
7. Usted
8. Tú

EXERCISE 99

1. viejo
2. nuevo
3. grande
4. pequeño

EXERCISE 100

bueno buena
malo mala
divertido divertida
delicioso deliciosa
alto alta
bajo baja

EXERCISE 101

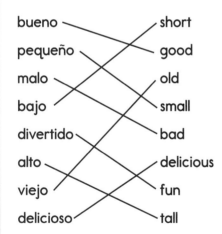

bueno — good
pequeño — small
malo — bad
bajo — short
divertido — fun
alto — tall
viejo — old
delicioso — delicious

EXERCISE 102

1. viejo
2. grande
3. delicioso
4. bajo

5. divertido
6. pequeño
7. malo
8. nueva

EXERCISE 103

1. el postre
2. el helado
3. la galleta
4. el pastel

EXERCISE 104

1. la bebida
2. la leche
3. el jugo
4. el agua

EXERCISE 105

1. el pastel
2. el jugo
3. el agua
4. la galleta
5. la leche
6. el helado

EXERCISE 106

1. el agua
2. la leche
3. el jugo
4. el helado
5. el pastel
6. el postre

EXERCISE 107

An image of a table with a blue pitcher of water, a white carton of milk, a brown cookie, a yellow piece of cake, an orange glass of juice, and a green soft drink

EXERCISE 108

Answers will vary.

EXERCISE 109

la casa
la puerta
la ventana
la cocina
la estufa
el tenedor
el cuchillo
la cuchara
el vaso

EXERCISE 110

el dormitorio
la cama
la almohada
la manta
la lámpara
el baño
la ducha
la toalla
el jabón

EXERCISE 111

image of a bedroom   el tenedor
image of a bar of soap   la puerta
image of a fork   la toalla
image of a towel   la cama
image of a spoon   la cuchara
image of a door   el dormitorio
image of a bed   la ducha
image of a shower   el jabón

EXERCISE 112

1. la lámpara
2. la manta
3. el dormitorio
4. la almohada
5. la ducha
6. el tenedor
7. la estufa
8. la cuchara

EXERCISE 113

1. el cuchillo
2. la cuchara
3. el vaso
4. la almohada
5. la cama
6. la ventana
7. la puerta
8. la casa
9. el baño
10. el jabón

EXERCISE 114

Answers will vary.

EXERCISE 115

la calle
el auto
la biblioteca
la escuela
el mercado
el parque
el cine
el museo

EXERCISE 116

Image of a school
Image of a park
Image of a car
Image of a museum
Image of a library
Image of a movie theater
Image of a street
Image of a grocery store

EXERCISE 117

1. El auto es nuevo.
2. La escuela es divertida.
3. El parque es bueno.
4. El mercado es grande.
5. La calle es gris.
6. La biblioteca es vieja.
7. El museo es pequeño.

EXERCISE 118

Answers will vary.

EXERCISE 119

1. el parque
2. la escuela
3. la biblioteca
4. el mercado
5. el cine
6. el auto
7. la calle
8. el museo

EXERCISE 120

1. La calle es mala.
2. El museo es divertido.
3. La escuela es buena.
4. El auto es rosado.
5. El cine es nuevo.
6. El parque es viejo.
7. La biblioteca es roja.
8. El mercado es pequeño.

EXERCISE 121

el fútbol
el fútbol americano
el baloncesto
la natación
el béisbol
el baile
la lectura
la música

EXERCISE 122

Answers will vary.

EXERCISE 123

1. el béisbol
2. el baile
3. la natación
4. la lectura

5. el fútbol
6. el fútbol americano
7. el baloncesto
8. la música

EXERCISE 124

baseball image   soccer image
dancing image   football image
reading image   basketball image
music image   swimming image

EXERCISE 125

1. El baloncesto es bueno.
2. La natación es divertida.
3. El béisbol es nuevo.
4. El fútbol es viejo.
5. El baile no es malo.
6. La música es grande.

EXERCISE 126

Answers will vary.

EXERCISE 127

la maestra
el policía
el bombero
el médico
la enfermera
el veterinario

EXERCISE 128

el veterinario - image of a veterinarian
el médico - image of a doctor
el policía - image of a police officer
la enfermera - image of a nurse
la maestra - image of a teacher
el bombero - image of a firefighter

EXERCISE 129

Answers will vary.

EXERCISE 130

el médico
la maestra
el bombero
el veterinario
la enfermera
el policía

EXERCISE 131

el avión
el aeropuerto
el tren
el autobús
la playa
la montaña
la ciudad
el lago

EXERCISE 132

1. An image of a lake
2. An image of a mountain
3. An image of a city
4. An image of a beach
5. An image of a train
6. An image of an airport
7. An image of a bus
8. An image of an airplane

EXERCISE 133

la montaña
la playa
el tren
el lago
la ciudad
el autobús
el avión
el aeropuerto

EXERCISE 134

1. El lago es azul.
2. La montaña es alta.
3. La ciudad es grande.
4. La playa es buena.
5. El tren es rojo.
6. El aeropuerto es divertido.
7. El autobús es malo.
8. El avión es pequeño.

EXERCISE 135

1. el aeropuerto
2. el autobús
3. la ciudad
4. la montaña
5. la playa
6. el avión
7. el tren
8. el lago

EXERCISE 136

Answers will vary.

EXERCISE 137

1. ir
2. caminar
3. correr
4. jugar
5. gustar

EXERCISE 138

1. no gustar
2. hablar
3. comer
4. dormir
5. nadar

EXERCISE 139

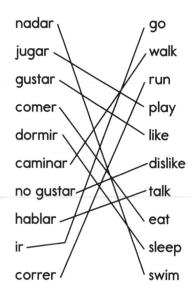

nadar — go
jugar — walk
gustar — run
comer — play
dormir — like
caminar — dislike
no gustar — talk
hablar — eat
ir — sleep
correr — swim

EXERCISE 140

1. nadar
2. hablar
3. dormir
4. caminar
5. comer
6. no gustar
7. correr
8. jugar
9. ir
10. gustar

EXERCISE 141

1. Drawing of a doctor not wanting to swim.
2. Drawing of a teacher running.
3. Drawing of a nurse eating an ice cream cone.
4. Drawing of a firefighter playing soccer.
5. Drawing of a policemen reading in the library.
6. Drawing of a veterinarian with a soap taking a bath.

EXERCISE 142

1. El museo es viejo.
2. La almohada es nueva.
3. El pastel es delicioso.
4. Hablar es bueno.
5. Jugar al béisbol es divertido.
6. La montaña es alta.
7. La maestra es baja.
8. El lago es pequeño.
9. El avión es grande.
10. El parque es malo.

EXERCISE 143

1. El cuchillo está en la cocina.
2. La ciudad es grande.
3. La ducha está en el baño.
4. Tú eres mi hermana.
5. Usted es mi médico.
6. La estufa está buena.
7. La manta está en el dormitorio.
8. El baile es divertido.
9. Me gusta ir a la playa para nadar.
10. El postre está en el mercado.

EXERCISE 144

Answers will vary.

About the Author

 **Melanie Stuart-Campbell** is also the author of *Alba, the South American Street Dog, Learn Spanish with Pictures,* and *A Spanish Workbook for Kids.* She is an instructional specialist and advocate for the Kansas Migrant Education Program, working with many people who celebrate Día de los Muertos. She also teaches online Spanish classes to kids on the website Outschool.

Melanie has been a teacher in Kansas, New York City, Ecuador, and the Republic of Congo. She lives in Kansas with her husband and two children, and serves on her local school board. You can see her other books on her website AlbasSpanishTales.com.